# 40 Days to a Prosperous Soul Devotional

## When You Know Your Purpose, It's Time to Unlock Your Abundance

*by*
*Thomas Weeks, III*

**Harrison House**
Tulsa, Oklahoma

09 08 07 06 05     10 9 8 7 6 5 4 3 2 1


*40 Days to a Prosperous Soul Devotional—*
*When You Know Your Purpose, It's Time to Unlock Your Abundance*
ISBN 1-57794-739-8
Copyright © 2005 by Thomas Weeks, III
Thomas Weeks, III Ministries
P.O. Box 60866
Washington, DC 20039

Published by Harrison House, Inc.
P.O. Box 35035
Tulsa, Oklahoma 74153

# CONTENTS

UNLOCK YOUR ABUNDANCE

# Introduction:

# A Prosperous Soul Prospers Abundantly

I love to read the story of Job because Job learned an invaluable lesson which provides us with the ability to discover the true source of power God gave mankind. After God restored Job's wealth in abundance, giving him twice as much as he had lost, Job learned his previous prosperity had been from a limited source of power. His family of seven sons and three daughters; material wealth of thousands of sheep and camels, hundreds of oxen and donkeys, and a very great body of servants—prosperity so vast that he was identified as "...the greatest of all the men of the East" (Job 1:2-3 AMP)—Job learned was from the *limited* prosperity of his own mind.

Job is one of the Bible examples of a soul prosperous in relationship with God prospering abundantly, a priority later described in Jesus' words:

> But seek (aim at and strive after) first of all His kingdom and His righteousness (His way of doing and being right), and then all these things taken together will be given you besides.
>
> Matthew 6:33 AMP

Through the soul (the mind, will, and emotions), we make the decisions and take the actions that bring us into closer relationship with God and determine the degree to which we avail ourselves of everything God intends for us to have.

This God-fearing man, Job, in walking through extremely difficult experiences, learned that mind prosperity is temporal; soul prosperity is eternal. The enemy, Satan, destroyed everything that represented Job's prosperity except for the intangible asset through which God funneled His abundance, Job's soul. God, *The* Source of true prosperity and all things good, who had created humanity to live from the soul as the source of prosperity in relationship with Him, protected Job's soul.

Job saw the importance of something his close friends lacked when he found himself lacking. God expanded Job's knowledge so that Job came to a pivotal realization: *You can possess everything in this material world and still not know the God you think you know.*

In the face of his friends' false accusations, presented as if God's view of the calamities resulted from Job's sins, Job maintained his innocence and integrity. He persevered in his trust in God to vindicate him, stating, "…when he has tested me, I will come forth as gold" (Job 23:10 NIV), and knew to wait until the change came. Job knew that he would come out of this experience as a *valued substance,* not one who places value on earthly substance. Clearly seeing his years of wealth as from the limited prosperity of his own mind, Job was learning to live from the wealth within his soul.

God did vindicate Job after first speaking to Job from a whirlwind, correcting Job for questioning Him, the Creator, as if He could be wrong or unjust! Job immediately repented, stating he had spoken of things he didn't understand.

Angry at Job's friends, God addressed them, "…you have not spoken of me what is right, as my servant Job has" (Job 42:7 NIV) and instructed them to go to Job and sacrifice a burnt offering for themselves. Job would pray for them, whose prayer He would accept. God turned back Job's captivity and gave him the capacity to possess double—first in his soul and then in the natural realm. With patience we possess our souls (Luke 21:19). A prosperous soul knows how to exercise patience, and from a prosperous soul the Lord is able to prosper us in every way. *Captivity is a place for capacity building.*

Consider each day of your journey through this devotional to be a fresh day of destiny. The number *forty* has great significance. Moses was on the mountaintop with God for forty days receiving revelation for an entire nation. Jesus was in the wilderness for forty days receiving power for a purpose that would change the world. I pray when these forty days are over, your spirit will be on the mountaintop of revelation concerning your destiny, and that the kingdom of God will be operating through your daily life with power to manifest a prosperous purpose.

There are greater depths in God with each day you learn to walk in soul prosperity. I hope that as you read you'll discover the priceless value of your soul. Let me encourage you to do something that will change your life forever. Never let a day go by without thanking God for the soul He gave you that can prosper abundantly in Christ...for this is your greatest possession.

# Day 1

## GOD INTENDED TRUE PROSPERITY FROM THE BEGINNING

> Beloved, I pray that you may prosper in every way and [that your body] may keep well, even as [I know] your soul keeps well and prospers.
>
> 3 John 2 AMP

God works through soul prosperity to perfom what He has promised. Soul prosperity is not about what we have, but who we are in Christ. It is the vehicle to our destiny and the key to abundant life right now. Yet, like our spiritual ancestors, we must choose the right path that will lead to true abundance.

God begins revealing how to develop a prosperous soul, and the true prosperity that results, in the first five books of the Old Testament. Especially through types and shadows of the redemptive, restorative work of His Son, Jesus, depicted later in the New Testament, God reveals to us how to prepare for and acquire prosperity and how to manage and use it to help us help others.

God created man to exercise dominion in the earth. From the beginning, God intended for true prosperity to be enjoyed by all His children. Through Jesus, we have the opportunity to be restored in relationship with God and live as God intended for us from the beginning.

After mankind fell and became separated from The Source of abundance by sin, Jesus came to earth to restore the connection for those who will believe in Him and the work He did. Jesus died on the cross as a sacrifice to take our sins upon Himself and provide forgiveness, then rose from the dead to provide the Way back to The Source of prosperity for us.

## Know Your Purpose

*Believe that God intends for you to prosper.*

# Day 2

## UNCOVERING THE DEEP MYSTERIES OF GOD

Wisdom is the principal thing; therefore get wisdom: and with all thy getting get understanding.

Proverbs 4:7

Prosperity…what does it really mean? How does it apply to your life? These are vital questions that you must address to fulfill your destiny in God. The wisdom you need is found through the eye of Scripture, where we learn how to prepare for, acquire, and manage biblical prosperity and wealth.

The Bible is written in three major dimensions: inspiration, revelation, and the prophetic. Prophetic revelation—because it is the highest level—unlocks the deep mysteries of God regarding true prosperity. But the prophetic code can be difficult to receive because it takes time and hard labor to gain deeper insight. Types and shadows as well as patterns and systems of numbers are prophetic forms to be discovered.

With this in mind, let me explain the basis of prophetic biblical numerology (at the heart of the code of prophetic interpretation). Prophetic patterns run throughout the Bible in the form of basic numbers. Each number has a specific meaning that becomes clearer the more you study and meditate upon the Word. **One** is whole: nothing needs to be added to it. **Two** represents divine agreement. **Three** is resurrection and completion. **Four** is the number of supernatural impartation. **Five** represents grace. **Six** is the number of man. **Seven** is the number of perfection. **Eight** represents new beginnings. **Nine** represents birthing. **Zero**, the number of eternity, is without end.

As you study prosperity in light of the prophetic code, you will gain a better understanding of how the Old Testament relates to the New Testament on this topic. Many of these devotions contain principles prophetically drawn from Genesis, Exodus, Leviticus, Numbers, and Deuteronomy. The remaining devotions will focus on accessing, acquiring, and activating God-given wealth principles in your life, based on truths God revealed to Joshua when he led a new generation of Israelites into the Promised Land.

Amos 3:7 says that God will do nothing without revealing it to His prophets, and I announce to you as a prophet of God that you've entered the prophetic realm. I pray these devotions will liberate your spirit to believe that prosperity is for you, especially when balanced with the understanding that your soul must prosper first. As your soul prospers by the impartation of the prophetic Word, prosperity in all its forms will be drawn to you like a magnet!

## Know Your Purpose

*Dwell on God's Word.*

# Day 3

## THE BIRTHPLACE OF SOUL PROSPERITY

### THE LAW OF CREATION: GENESIS

And God said, Let us make man in our image, after our likeness: and let them have dominion over…the earth. So God created man in his own image, in the image of God created he him; male and female created he them.

Genesis 1:26–27

It's pitch black, like midnight, and the waves are churning out of control. Something's moving—no, hovering—all around you. Everything seems like it's about to change for the worst. You cry, "No! This can't be happening to me!" Suddenly, everything turns upside down—again. Who got you into this mess? You're trying everything you know to find a path that will lead you into daylight, but it's too dark, too cold.

That black, churning chaos represents your life without a vital, living, breathing relationship with God. From the beginning He created you to be a living soul—full of life, joy, and abundance. Through Jesus Christ, you can find the real path to prosperity. And if you let Him guide you, this time it will be different.

This time you'll know that presence hovering above you is the Holy Spirit, and He's ready to begin God's work in you at the sound of the Father's voice. Now when each of those golden opportunities comes your way, you'll be ready to recognize and seize every one in order to maximize it to its full potential. Finally, you'll know who you are and where you are going—and your life will never be the same.

Like Adam's soul when he was created, your regenerated soul carries the absolute ability to reference God on every dimension—the historical, the now, and the future—all at the same time. You were born again into eternity and your soul is timeless. It is living. It is perfect. You received the breath of life from God Himself. And that breath was received into a vessel that had been broken by sin but was redeemed and brought into perfect communion with God.

When God breathed into Adam's nostrils, he received perfect abilities to exercise perfect dominion in the earth. God equipped him to prosper as he exercised his dominion over the earth. When Adam sinned, prosperity was lost—but not forever. God's creation would yield a return in the person of Jesus Christ.

Jesus' death and resurrection brought provision for restoring man—spirit, soul, and body—back together with God. After His resurrection, He appeared to His disciples and breathed on them (John 20:21–22) just like God had breathed into Adam. Then in Acts 2:4 they were filled with the Holy Spirit to accomplish the mission God had originally given to Adam.

True prosperity was restored to you when you were born again and filled with God's power. You became a living soul that is destined by God to prosper.

## Know Your Purpose

*You are destined by God to prosper.*

# Day 4

~~~

## YOUR SOUL RESTORED

And be not conformed to this world: but be ye transformed
by the renewing of your mind, that ye may prove what is that
good, and acceptable, and perfect, will of God.

Romans 12:2

Jesus is perfectly able to restore your soul. He knows you
better than you know yourself, and because He is the Word
(John 1:1,14), He can enter your soul through the Holy
Spirit—the heart of God—and release divine prosperity into
the natural realm *from the inside out*.

Adam lost the "eternal" aspect of his soul and spirit as part
of the curse in Genesis 3:19. And since God is a Spirit, Jesus
came to earth, completed the prophetic process, and then sent
the Holy Spirit to reconnect the "eternal" heart of God with
the mortal heart of man—to guide us back to the truth of
soul dominion.

When you have dominion over your soul (your mind, will,
and emotions) through renewing your mind to the Word
(Rom. 12:2 above), your soul is in agreement with your spirit,
the Holy Spirit, and the Word of God. And that kind of unity
brings the power and prosperity of God into your life.

God reunited the heart (spirit) and soul (brain)—mind,
will, and emotions—with Him through Jesus Christ, who, in

turn, released God's Spirit back into the earth to "fill" mortal hearts and restore man's original status as a *living soul*. In other words, you can have soul dominion as you obey the heart of God within you—that comes through the "completed" work of Jesus Christ and the "perfected" ministry of the Holy Spirit. Only as you abide in the Holy Spirit (i.e., the "breath of life") and receive directly from the heart of God into the heart of your soul will you be equipped to prosper, just like Adam.

Before He was crucified, Jesus prayed to the Father, "Neither pray I for these [disciples] alone, but for them also which shall believe on me through their word; that they all may be one.... I in them, and thou in me, that they may be made perfect in one; and that the world may know that thou hast sent me, and hast loved them, as thou hast loved me" (John 17:20-21,23).

As we go deeper into this prophetic revelation for true, biblical prosperity, I pray that your heart and mind will be "perfected" as a living soul, and that you will reclaim soul dominion according to God's original plan.

## *Know Your Purpose*

*The Lord restoreth my soul* (see Ps. 23:3).

# Day 5

### ~~~

# THE DAILY WALK OF YOUR SOUL

> For what shall it profit a man, if he shall gain the whole world,
> and lose his own soul?

Mark 8:36

After the new birth your soul doesn't need to search for God; it's already trying to seek Him because it knows the essence of your potential in Him. The dilemma comes when you have to go through what I call the "God test" to determine if you'll be accountable to walk in this soul dominion.

In Genesis 1:26–28, God gave Adam total dominion over all the earth and challenged him with the vital task of naming every animal (2:19). This was a great test of Adam's accountability. I believe this is one reason why the Bible records that God spoke with him on a consistent basis. In order for God to transfer His dominion over the earth to Adam, He had to establish a regular time of communion with him.

Jesus was the second Adam, and the Bible says He did only what He saw the Father doing (John 5:19). So it is reasonable to assume that Adam operated the same way in naming the animals. Would he name the animals exactly what God had called them? Obviously so. "That's a giraffe…an elephant…a hippopotamus…penguin…eagle…." God was able to use Adam's mouth to name the animals because his soul was perfect—it worked in the spiritual realm because of Adam's soul dominion: consciousness of God (spirit), consciousness of self (soul), and a revelational consciousness of the world (body).

Through Jesus Christ we again can live by the soul dominion God intended for us from the beginning. If we work from our soul being properly connected to God through renewing our mind to His Word and being led by His Spirit rather than by the flesh, our spirits will speak what comes from Him, and we will walk in soul dominion. We can reference God on every level if we exercise the prophetic dominion He's given us by vocalizing what we hear Him say.

It's like God was saying to Adam, "Whatever you decree by your voice when your soul is in dominion changes the atmosphere. Everything you speak will be as subject to your voice as it was to Mine. As your voice begins to name every creature exactly as I'd name them, I'll know My kingdom has come to the earth and My will shall be done in the earth through you. Speak, Adam, because your prosperity begins with ruling and having dominion over all living creatures. You're a living soul. You must have dominion over every living thing."

In Christ, you are a living snapshot of the eternal purpose of God!

## Know Your Purpose

*Through Jesus, we can be restored to the dominion God originally intended.*

# Day 6

*~~~*

## THE PROCESS OF SOUL PROSPERITY

> I have this day set thee over the nations and over the
> kingdoms, to root out, and to pull down, and to destroy, and
> to throw down, to build, and to plant.
>
> Jeremiah 1:10

If you hire a contractor to restore your hardwood floors, you don't want him to simply cover what's already there with shellac. He needs to sand down all the layers to get back to the original wood. And many times when God starts to deal with you about moving to another level, He has to sand down issues in your life so that you can see the person He originally created you to be.

Whenever God's in the process of doing something new in your life, He starts breaking down everything from the past. Rooting out, pulling down, destroying, and throwing down come before building and planting—especially when you are believing God for a new level of prosperity!

In the prophetic code, three is the number of resurrection and completeness: Jesus was raised on the third day, the Godhead is made up three persons, and so on. In Psalm 1:1-3, there are three references made to one who is blessed of God:

1. He walks not in the counsel of the ungodly.

2. Nor does he stand in the way of sinners.

3. Nor does he sit in the seat of the scornful.

First, the "blessed" believer's body demonstrates righteousness, not ungodly imaginations. You can usually tell where people have been or where they're going by looking at how they walk. They're confident, timid, excited, depressed, joyful…or "hating on" someone. You're truly blessed when your body reflects the character of God.

The soul of a "blessed" believer doesn't get lifted up, think they are mature, or find fault with everybody else. So be careful. When you think you've "arrived," it becomes a sin to your soul. And don't assume everything's perfect just because God is using you! When you start to think you're so great at something, get ready for the effects of pride to break you down.

In your spirit, you need to know God for yourself so that He can help you make it through life's tests. Don't hide from Him like Adam and Eve when they committed sin. And your grandmother may know God, but her faith in God can't always deliver you. Also, human opinions can't take you to another level—only God can do this. There are some things He has ordained that you can take only to Him.

Most important, once you come out of your "night season" of being broken down and being on your face communing with Him, you'll have a signed guarantee that something new is about to happen in your life.

## Know Your Purpose

*Breaking down and rooting out areas of the past that cause you to lose ground clear the way to build and plant a prosperous future.*

# Day 7

<img — decorative rule>

## DELIGHTING IN THE LORD'S WORD

But his delight is in the law of the Lord; and in his law doth he
meditate day and night.

Psalm 1:2

A "new day" literally begins as your soul delights in the law
of the Lord, causing you to become everything He created you
to be. When you come to delight in Him, you understand that
being in the center of His will strengthens you. Did you come
out of a hard situation with more power, greater peace, deeper
commitment, and a greater testimony and understanding of
who God is in you and what you're supposed to do in God?
Then you've entered a new day of delight.

Psalm 1:3 says, "And he shall be like a tree...that bringeth
forth his fruit in his season...." When God tells you it's your
time and season, the joy of the Lord will carry you into your
destiny. It will literally possess you to do all that your heart
desires. Your soul will overflow with noble passion and the
devil won't be able to come near you—because he was never
anointed to do what you are doing.

You are "blessed" by God because you've delighted in His
Word day and night, and God will overshadow you until you
become the person of His original design. He's going to guide
you where you need to go in order to get what you need to

have. He's going to be your eyes so you'll see clearly—His view according to His Word.

Times couldn't have been worse for the disciples when they were paralyzed with fear after Jesus' crucifixion. *They were in pitch darkness.* Then Jesus stood in their midst, overshadowed them, and revealed His total victory. The secret place is the place of revelation, the place of your assignment. And believe me, joy will come in the morning.

As long as it looks dark around you, you're in His shadow! Don't be swayed by superficial things. Don't try to merely satisfy yourself with happiness. Seek for joy. And when it's dark, press in deeper to His presence. Go deeper in His shadow, and you'll be transformed even more by His image. When everything is bright and clear, you have to look for His shadow and stay there. God won't unveil you until He's finished "performing" His Word in your life in the particular area He's working to transform.

Your soul is always qualified by the proof of what you've experienced in God. And I'm not talking about a song, a shout, and a sermon. I'm talking about delighting in God, even when you're under His shadow...especially when you're there, because after it's all said and done, only those (supernatural) things which can't be shaken will remain.

## Know Your Purpose

*Bringing forth fruit will carry you into your destiny.*

# Day 8

## THE PROCESS OF SOUL PERFORMANCE

Well done, thou good and faithful servant: thou hast been faithful over a few things, I will make thee ruler over many things: enter thou into the joy of thy lord.

Matthew 25:21

In Matthew 25:14–30, the parable of the talents, one servant received five talents, another two talents, and another one. Their master gave each the opportunity to prosper. Interestingly, the one with five and the one with two seized the divine opportunity and realized their fullest potential, increasing according to their own ability. The servant with one talent buried it.

I think this reflects where the church is today. We look at what we have through unprospering souls, and our lack of understanding causes us to cancel our own multiplication process. What has it profited the body of Christ to gain the whole world (get people saved) but never accomplish what we were destined to do—build the kingdom?

Maybe some have buried the prosperity message because they don't believe they can live in the supernatural power of God. But He wants us to live, move, and have our being in Him. Salvation is using our God-given talents to increase, multiply, and receive in abundance. If my soul only desires to have a heavenly experience and is content to wait until I get to heaven to know, see, hear, and be blessed by God—then why is God prophetically saying through this parable that our faithfulness yields rich rewards in this life? Why is He showing us it includes material blessings, multiplication in our professions, and most importantly, receiving His supernatural joy?

No matter where you are today, financially or otherwise, you can't lose as long as you endeavor to prosper what God has given you. The servant that buried his talent couldn't enter into the joy of the Lord because he believed God was a wicked taskmaster and prosperity was wicked. He would rather receive a limited measure of talents on a regular basis than to use what was in his hands to multiply his potential for increase. God called *him* wicked!

God's prosperity comes only when you choose to operate in His purpose. Jesus already gave you the "breath of life" and empowered you with supernatural ability to utilize every talent and opportunity God has placed within you. Your miracle increase is resting in your own hands.

The voice of the Lord is coming to you from the cool of the Garden…will you hearken unto Him and obey? Will your soul prosper by walking in His image and likeness? When you do, you will come into alignment with God's original purpose and set yourself up for divine increase. That is the Law of Creation seen in the process of soul performance.

## Know Your Purpose

*Prosper what God has given you.*

# Day 9

*~~~~~*

## CATAPULTING INTO A FUTURE BEYOND YOUR DREAMS

### THE LAW OF EXPANSION: EXODUS

As the hart [deer] panteth after the water brooks, so panteth
my soul after thee, O God. My soul thirsteth for God, for the
living God....

Psalm 42:1–2

Soul understanding operates on different dimensions: It
touches the reality of who (we know) we are in truth, what we
desire for the future (because it understands that eternal desire
is birthed in God), and also where we've been with God. The
soul understands the legacy of the spirit realm that births us
into the anointing we're experiencing right now, so it seeks to
protect this anointing—and our future destiny—by gently
keeping us aware that we must communicate consistently with
the Lord. This is how we come into expansion.

Continuing on the path to abundant living by walking the
"length" and "breadth" of the land like Abraham, we maintain
a deep, abiding relationship with the Lord. This is how
Abraham was able to walk in newness of life and pass a
righteous lineage down to future generations—to expand.

In the book of Exodus Moses was required to turn and walk
toward God. In doing so, he became the prophetic prototype for

our souls to begin to "pant after" God. When Moses' season came—after being adopted by Pharaoh's daughter, murdering an Egyptian soldier, fleeing for fear of his life from Egypt, and living in the desert for forty years in Midian—God called him.

God said, "Now Moses, this burning bush represents My presence. You're going to step on holy ground as you come close to Me. Take off your shoes, Moses, because I need you to come before Me with nothing between us like Adam was bare before Me. Wherever you walk I'll be with you, because I'm going to be with your soul. I AM THAT I AM."

This is how the book of Exodus brings us into expansion. You can't come into divine revelation and not reach beyond what you've always known. Divine revelation places a demand on you to change. And if it changed Moses, it can also change you. Understand something: God didn't call out to Moses until He saw that Moses had "turned aside to see" why the bush wasn't burned (Ex. 3:4). Moses turned around, started walking toward God, and then he was brought into revelation. Do you see the prophetic principle?

Revelation is the light of eternity. That is why the bush was never consumed. And the Holy Spirit is the fire of God within you that can change your atmosphere by revelation, if you obey. Your everyday life can be flooded with a brilliant light from heaven that's so majestic, everything will change—because of the eternal expansion in your soul.

## Know Your Purpose

*Obey the Lord to expand into the future He has for you.*

# Day 10

## BECOME WHO YOU ARE— AND RECEIVE WHAT YOU HAVE

The thief cometh not, but for to steal, and to kill, and to destroy: I am come that they might have life, and that they might have it more abundantly.

John 10:10

Here's a prophetic code principle: You'll never prosper in the fullness of God if you cling to limited experiences that are traditional in their inception, conception, and reality of experience. When God gave Moses divine insight, his lack of self-esteem caused him to react abnormally. He did not believe he was the man God thought he was. If you're going to prosper, you must believe you already are what God says you'll become.

The clarion call that resides in every soul is this: Whenever I AM has come, there must be expansion. If you're ordained to be wealthy, you must say it before it comes to pass. Remember how God created the heaven and the earth and declared, "I am a great entrepreneur…I am prospering in my own business…I am wealthy…I am a networker…I am empowered with education," and so on. When you decree I AM, you're referencing God on another dimension and ready to prosper in true abundance.

Because you've already become what God has destined you to be, you already have what He has promised. Believer, you can only prosper to the measure that you believe you'll prosper. So let me encourage you. God just wants you to recognize that you can start decreeing you are what He's created you to be already. Jesus came to give you abundant life, but you must decree it to receive it—and then you must move forward to take it.

I've been an entrepreneur since I was nine years old. I enjoyed the perspective of knowing that wealth was supposed to come to me because I always worked hard. One day I started my own lawn service. On the first day I made eighteen dollars cutting grass around the neighborhood. When I got back home, my father had my mother call me into the kitchen. I'll never forget it.

She sat me down at the table and said, "Son, I'm going to teach you the best way to be the greatest businessman you could ever be, and that is to honor God." Out came my tithe, an offering, reimbursement for all the supplies I had used to do the job, and savings. Honoring God was not just tithing but doing the right—and wise—thing.

This wisdom transformed my life and took me to another level of prosperity because I became a covenant keeper. I expanded into covenant with my God and with those who helped me, mentored me, and inspired me. I began to think and act as the person God intended me to be.

### Know Your Purpose

*You will become the greatest businessperson*
*you could ever be by honoring God.*

# Day 11

HAVING YOUR BEING IN HIM

And when Joshua heard the noise of the people as they shouted,
he said unto Moses, There is a noise of war in the camp.

Exodus 32:17

If you give God His tithe, that 10 percent, He will turn
around and give you what you couldn't get without Him.

There were times when I did not honor God and stay in
covenant. One day in church somebody gave me a $3.00
offering to celebrate my birthday. I went straight to the candy
store, slapped that $3.00 on the counter, and said, "Give me
300 pieces of candy." Well, I got cavities and my parents' dental
bill was horrific. You see, I didn't give God His tithe.

The same thing happened to the children of Israel. God had
told Moses it was time to establish some guidelines for their
new, prosperous future. He revealed the covenant laws (Ex.
20–23), how they could walk in heavenly authority on earth. I
can hear Him saying, "Children, this is a new day. I've delivered
you from bondage, given you supernatural food and water, and
now I want to show you more of who I AM by teaching you how
to live, move, and have your being in Me. Whatever you do
from this day forward, always abide in Me, and you can walk in
the ways of My heavenly kingdom on earth."

The glory of the Lord covered Mount Sinai for six days. But the children of Israel saw a devouring fire because after forty days, when Moses came down with his servant, Joshua, Israel had fallen into sin. When Moses and Joshua came down from the mountain, Joshua said prophetically, "There is a noise of war in the camp" (Ex. 32:15,17).

You see, they'd had an anointed worship service, heard the Word of the Lord, and made the proper sacrifices—so why was God taking so long to do what He had to do? This time they didn't want to wait on the Lord like Moses did, so they persuaded Aaron to make a golden calf, and they had an idolatrous celebration (Ex. 32:18–19).

Sin has a price. Three thousand souls were killed by the sword that day. When you are expanded by God you must not fail to weigh the consequences of disobedience. I withheld my tithe from God and heard the noise of war three months later when I grew too fast and didn't have money to get new clothes. I prayed for help and God showed me His tithe in candy!

The people of Israel held that first sacrifice and offering in disdain. We both paid a price. God is good, but if we stop walking His path to abundance, we can delay or abort His blessings. Honor God, stay in covenant, and avoid the noise of war!

## Know Your Purpose

*Keep walking the Lord's path to abundance.*

# Day 12

COMING INTO THE PROMISE

Bring ye all the tithes into the storehouse, that there may be meat in mine house, and prove me now herewith, saith the LORD of hosts, if I will not open you the windows of heaven, and pour you out a blessing, that there shall not be room enough to receive it.

Malachi 3:10

Tithing as an act of obedience and your offering as a sacrifice are the keys to prosperity. Tithing is 10 percent of your income; it doesn't change. It's an equal sacrifice for the one that makes a million dollars a week or a hundred dollars a week.

A lot of preachers say, "Come and *pay* God your tithes." But the book of Malachi tells you to *bring* your tithes. When you bring something to someone, you're honoring them. When you pay someone, it means you owe them something. Let me deposit something into your spirit: Bringing your tithes celebrates who God is; it honors Him because you have to be prepared to bring.

I have found that people who bring tithes begin to operate in a manifested level of experience with the Lord. They begin to see the windows of heaven opened in every area of their lives. Listen. God can pour out such rich blessings in your life that you'll feel you can't receive any more! It will boggle your mind when He showers you on every side. And you'll become a testimony that whatever God has ordained will come to pass.

Your offering represents the covenant of your prosperity. You can never prosper above the level of your offerings. For example, if you make a thousand dollars a week and give God two dollars as an offering after you tithe, it's because you've chosen to prosper at Saks Fifth Avenue, Wal-Mart, or some other place—instead of prospering in God.

The next time you go to the house of God, decree in covenant with Him that as you begin to expand, as you become the person He's ordained you to be, that you'll prepare Him an offering—because whoever the I AM is in your soul will always be represented by the type of offering you present. If you present a small offering, you have a small understanding of I AM…if you give a generous offering, you have a deeper understanding of I AM.

God presented Cain with a significant opportunity when He challenged him (in so many words), "Cain, if you don't do right according to who you know I AM, then 'sin lieth at the door'" (Gen. 4:7). But Cain rejected the counsel of God, which brings us back to the law of expansion. Your soul can only expand as much as you're willing to be taught.

God can teach you how to give an acceptable offering. He can show you how to give your best in order to expand and to keep on expanding!

## Know Your Purpose

*Your soul will expand according to your willingness to be taught.*

# Day 13

## PROPER PLANNING, EXECUTION, AND DISCIPLINE

### THE LAW OF DIVINE ORDER: LEVITICUS

To every thing there is a season, and a time to every purpose
under the heaven: A time to be born, and a time to die; a time
to plant, and a time to pluck up that which is planted.

Ecclesiastes 3:1–2

One of the first things you begin to learn from God as you
walk His path to abundance is that there's a time, a season, and
a purpose for everything. And if you really come into an
understanding of this, you'll develop a balanced perspective,
which leads to a healthy, balanced life. Things will change—
especially as you walk with God—because He's going to bring
you into divine order.

God is a God of order. He always has a purpose and a plan,
and His plan always comes to pass. There were eight steps in
the process of creation. *Seven* of them set the stage for man's
arrival...*perfect* order. So what should we look like? What
image should we project? Ephesians 5:1 says we should imitate
our Father.

Here's a prophetic principle: If you want to look like your
Father, and if you want to come into true abundance, you have
to apply proper planning and execution. God didn't just throw

His prized creation into a swirling, black hole. He took every painstaking step of preparation to make sure everything was in place. Then He created man. Get the picture?

We have examined the Law of Creation in Genesis, the Law of Expansion in Exodus, and now we're looking into the Law of Divine Order in Leviticus. When God liberated Israel from bondage, He prospered them abundantly—but the people still had a slave mentality. They had to learn how to become truly rich by prospering their souls. Then God taught them how to manage and multiply what He'd bestowed upon them. This set the groundwork for the giving of the tithe, which could only be done through a priestly order.

Here's another prophetic principle: Divine Order, being able to present that which is ordained of God back to God, brings you into balance. Whatever God gives you in increase, a part of it should return to Him—and the rest of it should be used in a way that glorifies Him! This is the lesson He taught the children of Israel by establishing the priestly order.

Prior to the Exodus, Israel had become so absorbed in Egyptian culture, they'd lost the respect of how to approach God; so God established a priestly order to heighten their awareness of Him. He wanted His people to know that He was living in the midst of them and understood their needs and responsibilities. He established the priesthood to demonstrate the law of divine order and bring balance and health.

## Know Your Purpose

*Observe the time, season, and purpose.*

# Day 14

WHO YOU ARE TO BECOME

But seek ye first the kingdom of God, and his righteousness;
and all these things shall be added unto you.

Matthew 6:33

Seek ye *first*…priorities. Divine order brings you into a
new level of discipline. This is why certain things must stop,
because God doesn't want you to continue doing things the
wrong way. He has to put a divine pause in your life until you
learn to do things the right way, which is why the Israelites
came to a stop in the book of Leviticus—for one year at the
base of Mount Sinai.

Discipline must come because God's Word concerning you
must come to pass. Discipline is an essential part of change,
because it not only concerns who you are, it deals with who
you are to become. Many of us fail during spiritual Boot Camp,
when God is simply trying to bring our lives into divine order.
Then we wonder why we can't *name it and claim it!*

Just as a drill sergeant opens his mouth and yells, "Wake
up!" and gives the order to march—so would the priest in the
new Levitical order. They would sound a clarion call;
prophesy; announce the new, divine order and prosperity of
God; and assess the giftings and abilities of God's people.

Discipline is a fundamental resource. It cannot be a haphazard, once-in-a-while experience of a believer. It's a tool to manage your lifestyle that will remain at the forefront of what you desire to become in God; because God can only use people that have discipline in character, personality, perspective, planning, time, resources, energy, and communication. These people will bless His kingdom above measure.

The role of the priesthood was to bring divine correction, clarity, and conciseness into people's daily lives. And as the priests brought divine order between God and man, God began to bring divine order between man and his possessions. Seek ye first…priorities. Seek ye first…a list of things that must be accomplished after the first thing. Seek ye first…then second, then third, then fourth, then fifth…shall be added to you.

If you can seek first—Number 1—the King's domain, discipline, and divine order; looking for the King's entry into His assets (how He acquires and manages them); if you can get that in your spirit first, then all these "other" things that the Gentiles seek (money, food, drink, clothes) will be bestowed upon you by God Himself! Understanding divine order (discipline) releases the truth of the kingdom in your life and advances you to another level—a higher dimension in God.

## Know Your Purpose

*Discipline is a fundamental resource.*

# Day 15

## USING POTENTIAL AND OPPORTUNITIES

He becometh poor that dealeth with a slack hand: but the
hand of the diligent maketh rich.

Proverbs 10:4

Here's a prophetic principle: Potential and opportunities will
always present themselves, but your level of discipline will equate
what becomes true about the real you. The real you is already
in your soul. However, you can become poor by dealing with a
slack hand and undisciplined thinking. You can lose untold
riches by having an undisciplined lifestyle and attitude. "Oh,
whenever I get to it, next time, some other day...." Whenever
you start letting this come into your thought life, you've
minimized the level of abundance God can bring into your life.

Remember the parable of the talents? The servants with
five and two doubled their portions, and the one who hid just
one lost it. God sends power to the servants that are
disciplined enough to go out and not waste time. Many of us
want to do good, but we're not faithful. We can always be
consistent to a certain degree, but being faithful means to be
consistent *even when you don't feel like it.*

You have to recognize something about disciplined people:
They understand that how they treat God and the things that

pertain to Him ultimately identifies how He's going to treat them. In other words, you can't have dysfunction in your life and expect God to give you real prosperity—no matter how much you claim it, quote it, or say it.

If you can't keep your own car trunk clean, how can God trust you to transport an important package from one place to another? How you manage your closet space generally reflects in other areas—because if your closet's dysfunctional, your life is probably the same way. If you have difficulty identifying problems and putting them together, maybe it's because your closet's telling you something. It's hard for you to find things when you need them.

This is an extremely practical and insightful analogy as it concerns your spiritual maturity; because when you can't find what you need, you tend to go without. We lack because we lack the ability to be on time, to manage finances, to manage goals and desires. We lack discipline and divine order.

Why don't we just take the time to organize our lives so we'll know how much money we have? If we can get divine order into our souls, then we'll automatically achieve a greater level in God. As poverty is a spirit that lives through a lifestyle, so is the lifestyle of a person that becometh rich, who has obtained it because they've applied discipline.

## Know Your Purpose

*Your level of discipline will equate what*
*becomes true about the real you.*

# Day 16

## How to Become Rich

Ye shall do my judgments, and keep mine ordinances, to walk therein: I am the LORD your God.

Leviticus 18:4

I acquired a 54,000-square-foot complex to start our ministry. The grounds were overgrown, and weeds and broken glass were everywhere. Having started with no members, no money, and just a big vision, I began to sweep and clean up the broken glass, cut the weeds, and so on. I found pennies all over the ground: rusted, dirty, almost unrecognizable pennies. As I began to pick them up, I neatly stacked them in the windowsill in my office. Then I rolled them together and deposited them in the bank.

After a few months of this I attended a conference. I saw a shiny penny on the ground, bent down to pick it up, and God said, *Don't pick up the penny.* I picked it up…in disobedience to God. As I walked around the corner, the penny slipped out of my hand and rolled under a truck. When I knelt down to reach for it, God said, *If you pick up this penny this time, you'll pick up the spirit of poverty.*

I stared at that penny, then I stood up, let that penny lay there underneath the truck, and asked God what He was doing. He said, *For a season, you had to pick up pennies because they were there, but it wasn't part of your divine order, and I don't want you to form roots in that spirit. Pennies carry the spirit of poverty.*

I returned to the conference to find a person waiting. He said, "About forty-five minutes ago, God told me to write this check and give it to you." I thanked him and opened the envelope. It was a check for one thousand dollars! Obedience is always better than sacrifice!

Rich deals with lifestyle management more than how many things you have. Poor deals with the lack of lifestyle management. The abundant soul will acquire much, and a soul that's lacking will experience poverty. Remember the talents: "For unto every one that hath shall be given…but from him that hath not shall be taken away even that which he hath" (Matt. 25:29). Let's take it a little bit further. He that hath a soul of abundant living, or a living soul, shall have those things in life. He that hath not a living soul, or a life of abundance, shall lack those things in life.

The person who has learned discipline, seeks first the kingdom of God, and obeys the Word of the Lord, is a person who is truly rich. They understand and practice the law of divine order.

## Know Your Purpose

*Rich or poor deals with lifestyle management.*

# Day 17

~~~

## Proper Order and Consistently Accounted For

### The Law of Accountability: Numbers

Awake thou that sleepest, and arise from the dead, and Christ
shall give thee light. See then that ye walk circumspectly, not as
fools, but as wise, redeeming the time, because the days are evil.

Ephesians 5:14–16

As you continue down the path to soul prosperity, it won't
be long before you come to the place of *accountability*—
because your soul must be accountable to God. It came from
Him, so it must present itself back to Him. The question is: Do
you know exactly what's in your soul? Have you *awakened to*
the resources He's given you to maximize your potential?

You must learn to become accountable for your own soul
prosperity. When the book of Numbers begins, we find God
speaking to Moses two years after Israel was delivered from
Egypt (Num. 1:1). *Two* is the number of *agreement*—so
becoming accountable to God puts you into agreement with
Him…and that's powerful.

Israel completed construction of the Tabernacle in Exodus,
established the priesthood in Leviticus, and then God had a
place of rest among His people. There was the Outer Court
(where everyone could enter), the Holy Place (where only

priests could enter), and the Most Holy Place (where the ark of God rested behind the veil). At each level there came a new level of accountability—and a new intimacy with God.

God gives you a living soul, or soul dominion, through receiving Jesus Christ and the indwelling presence of the Holy Spirit. Then He leads you into the expansion of possessing the power of His name, I AM. So you come into the responsibility of a deeper relationship with God by submitting to the Holy Spirit, which gives you supernatural power to decree the things of God in the face of your enemies. Then the kingdom of God can be released in the earth through the Holy Spirit in you.

In Numbers 1:5, something significant was spoken to Moses: "And these are the names of the men that shall stand with you." Could there have been a divine connection between those who gave willingly and those who would stand with Moses? I think so. The men who had proven themselves to be faithful to diligently build God's house were then chosen to represent their tribe to all of Israel.

The Law of Accountability deals with integrity. This is why God simply won't allow your soul to remain in unfruitful places. So slow down, take time to digest the Word of God, lay yourself before Him in prayer and intercession—and then live responsibly outside of your prayer closet. Then your inner life will create a match with your outer expression.

### Know Your Purpose

*Recognize every divine deposit received from God,*
*and be able to present each one back to Him.*

# Day 18

## The Law of Trustworthiness

And they assembled all the congregation together on the first
day of the second month.... As the LORD commanded Moses,
so he numbered them in the wilderness of Sinai.

*Numbers 1:18-19*

The Law of Accountability also brings me into the Law of
Trustworthiness. If I can't be trusted, then I don't have the
integrity to embrace the full abundance of God. When you
come into abundance, you're accountable for everything that
happens in you, through you, for you, and by you. This is
impossible if you are not trustworthy.

You become accountable and trustworthy by handling your
finances wisely. If God is going to trust you, He wants to know
that you're managing your money right. For example, if I asked
you how much money you had in your wallet when you woke
up this morning, would you be able to tell me? Do you
maintain an accurate daily accounting of how much money is
in your checking, savings, or money market accounts?

God wants to make sure that, even though you may spend
it, you know where your money goes and why. The Law of
Accountability justifies this: "The reason why I did this is
because that needed to be taken care of." It references through
the book of Numbers that I should know where my increases

occur and why. Prosperity doesn't come by haphazard confession but from wise management, knowing where every penny came from and where every penny is going.

Can you count the actual cost of launching that new bicycle business? Can you gain perspective of what you're going to be able to generate from that computer when you buy it—or is it just going to be another idle machine in your house that has no value after two weeks?

Let's say you've been looking for tools. You bought a set last year, but now you can't find any of them. What happened? Did you leave the kit outside after you fixed the lawnmower? Did you forget where the ladder was until it rusted because you forgot to put it back?

The prophetic principle of Numbers has been identified: When the children of Israel were about to enter into another level and glory in God, it was because they knew how to give God His "numbers."

Some things may seem small but are extremely important. For example, how many times do you go shopping in a week, how much money do you spend on gas, how much extra time do you have? Certain things must be accounted for in order for you to prove trustworthy for God's blessings, which bring responsibility. You cannot achieve true success and abundance unless you are trustworthy.

## Know Your Purpose

*Be accountable and trustworthy by handling your finances wisely.*

# Day 19
_~~~~_

## AN ACCOUNTABLE SOUL WITH
## GOD AS THE SOURCE

O taste and see that the LORD is good: blessed is the man that
trusteth in him.

Psalm 34:8

When your soul is unaccountable, it can easily fall into
sin—and then to make matters worse, you camouflage it. Take
gambling, for example. Is that being accountable for numbers?
If someone says, "Oh, I wasn't really gambling; I was just
trying to win some money," and gives their whole paycheck to
buy lottery tickets—that's gambling!

Now, if you were to buy something at a rummage sale for
five dollars and, in turn, got a raffle ticket; then you waited
around for a drawing, that's not gambling. That's investing in an
opportunity. On the other hand, if this same five dollars were
your tithes or bill money, that's when it would become sin.

The point is, when your soul is unaccountable, your
actions can become uncontrollable—because they're dictated
by the ungodly passions in your soul. These become bad
habits, which shape circumstances with negative consequences.
If you've got a gambling addiction, that bad habit will have
you sitting there every day thinking, *Just five dollars…five more
dollars,* while you keep missing the numbers.

Gambling is a trust issue. God is no longer your Source. When you gamble compulsively, you've made the "opportunity" more "god" than God Himself. You don't trust Him enough to pay your tithes, and you throw your money away on chance.

Maybe you gamble with relationships. When you see a man you're attracted to, you think, *Let me just go over there and see what he says today.* You want to test that brother out, make something happen, but you won't admit that you don't trust God to bring you a mate.

We can also gamble with time. Let's say you pay $80 a month for cable. Are you counting the numbers? Let me help you. Eighty dollars a month divided by thirty days is approximately $2.50 a day (sixty cents an hour) to spend four to six hours in front of the television. How much is your time worth? Are you addicted? Essentially, there's nothing wrong with television, and you could turn sixty cents an hour into a lot more if you watch the right programs. But be accountable—always crunch the numbers.

Begin to assess everything in your life and know why it happens. Then stay accountable to God as your Source. When you know how to taste and see that the Lord is good, that He can be trusted with every issue of your life, God will bless you for it. And trusting Him will keep your soul from becoming a slave to ungodly passions.

## Know Your Purpose

*Be accountable by beginning to assess the cause and effect of everything that happens in, through, for, and by you.*

# Day 20

## God Is the Source of the Blessings

> Humble yourselves in the sight of the LORD, and he shall lift you up.
>
> James 4:10

In December 1997, I was preparing to pastor my church, and the Lord told me that He really wanted to sharpen some things in my life. So I went to a hotel and shut myself in. Some of my greatest weaknesses and strengths came to light.

Then the Lord asked me to count up as much debt as I could, and I ended up in a three-day shut-in, writing down every area of indebtedness. I didn't know that by the time I returned home, someone would inquire, "Tell me how much debt you're in," and after I stated the figure, pay off all of my debt. I believe God orchestrated this because I already had accountability. I knew exactly to the penny what was owed. Know the numbers!

This episode also points to another prophetic principle in Numbers regarding accountability: When you become aware of who you are in God and all He's given you, don't fall into pride. Aaron and Miriam spoke against Moses when he married an Ethiopian woman (Num. 12:1), "Hath the LORD indeed spoken only by Moses? hath he not spoken also by us?

And the LORD heard it" (v. 2). When we think too much of ourselves because of the blessings God has bestowed, He's obligated to set the record straight. Miriam was struck with leprosy and had to remain outside of the camp for seven days (Num. 12:10–15).

Pride is deceptive, because by Numbers 16 a revolt was brought against Moses by Korah, Dathan, and Abiram—priests in the Levitical order. They brought 250 leaders with them. "Ye take too much upon you, seeing all the congregation are holy, every one of them, and the LORD is among them: wherefore then lift ye up yourselves above the congregation of the LORD?" (Num. 16:3).

*Now take note.* Each of these people knew exactly who they were and what their position in God afforded them. And they had counted every reason why they should be favored like Moses—only they'd forgotten…God is a God of order. So He caused the earth to swallow up the entire tribe of Korah along with their possessions (Num. 16:28–33). God judged them for their pride.

Never try to rise above your assignment. Let God lift you up as the Bible says in James 4:10. Walk humbly in the Law of Accountability. And most of all, learn to count your blessings and give all the glory to God, because He's getting ready to lead you into divine increase.

## Know Your Purpose

*Function within your assignment.*

# Day 21

## God's Image Re-formed in You

### The Law of Increase and Overflow: Deuteronomy

Now unto him that is able to do exceeding abundantly above all that we ask or think, according to the power that worketh in us, Unto him be glory in the church by Christ Jesus throughout all ages....

Ephesians 3:20–21

In Genesis you witnessed the creative abundance of being a living soul in Christ, in Exodus you were expanded by experiencing God as I AM, God brought you into the divine order of discipline in Leviticus, and then He dealt with accountability and integrity in Numbers. Now you come to Deuteronomy, which speaks of divine increase and overflow. God expects you to walk consistently in His commandments until His image is re-formed in you—until you come into complete soul dominion and possess your rightful inheritance.

This is how you learn to access God on every level—by consistently identifying His voice within your soul and being obedient to Him, even when it seems impossible. I compare Deuteronomy to due diligence because Israel had to apply what God had taught them to possess the fullness of His promises.

There was a shift in leadership and focus in Deuteronomy. Moses had led a people who'd been blessed with abundance into discipline and accountability, to make them rich in their souls. Joshua would lead the next generation across the Jordan into wealth. Rich applies to individual growth, but wealth transforms a nation. Israel was going to a new level.

A person becomes rich by focusing on one area of worth, value, or abundance. A nation acquires wealth, which is generated by a collective effort on multiple levels, by utilizing resources to their fullest potential. God gives you the power to get wealth through networking amongst people with extraordinary vision, establishing diverse relationships, and building collective power or ability to increase beyond individual effort.

In Deuteronomy, Israel comes out of selfish and sinful worship into national covenant with God. So God moved Israel into collective wealth by refocusing them on what He'd said in the past: "For if ye shall diligently keep all these commandments...ye shall possess greater nations and mightier than yourselves" (Deut. 11:22–23).

Here's a powerful prophetic principle: A generational blessing is always released when you respect a covenant. God's not going to grant a generational blessing to people who look out for number one. Each individual must be hearing, obeying, and diligently pursuing God *in relationship to those around them.*

Don't become deadlocked in the area of financial prosperity by not keeping *all* the commandments of the Lord. Layer them in your spirit so that God can thrust you into the next level of corporate responsibility and wealth. Avoid picking and choosing what you'll obey. Then you won't lose the opportunity to prosper, even as He deepens the prosperity of your inner man individually and corporately.

## *Know Your Purpose*

*Consistently identify the Lord's voice within*
*your soul and be obedient to Him.*

# Day 22

## THE VOICE OF THE INNER PROPHET

For as many as are led by the Spirit of God, they are the sons
of God. The Spirit itself beareth witness with our spirit, that
we are the children of God.

Romans 8:14,16

God warned Israel in Deuteronomy 13:1-4 that the true
prophets always lead you in obedience to His Word. Your inner
prophet—the voice of the Lord through the Holy Spirit—
quickens you to fear the Lord and have faith in His Word. But
there is also a false prophet, which seeks to lead you according
to the flesh.

In 1996 I found myself at a crossroads, and this issue made
the critical difference. I'd been living and ministering in
Wilmington, Delaware, for over fifteen years when I traveled
to Washington, D.C. It strangely felt like home, and when I
returned to Wilmington, I felt like I was just visiting. God had
taken a turn in my life, and I knew it. My inner prophet was
speaking that something had changed.

Every believer is built to recognize when God's about to do
something distinctive and mighty in his or her life. There's a
sudden shifting…one moment you have one focus, and the
next moment everything's different.

I began to drive around Washington looking at properties for sale or rent, observing the various levels of poverty, status, and potential in the city. One day the Lord said, *Call the school on Ridge Road.* When I called to get the number, the operator gave me the number of another school. They said there was space available for rent, and I was to contact the school district to request a meeting. As soon as I hung up the Lord said, *Call back and ask for the principal.* After I debated Him on this point, He said again, *Call back and ask for the principal.*

I called and asked to speak with the principal. I was told that the principal was overwhelmed because it had been confirmed the school was closing indefinitely. That was my signal!

I had had two prophets working in me that day—but I knew the voice of my Lord, I obeyed Him, and He showed me His will. If I had followed the false prophet like my flesh wanted to, I would have put the call off until later and missed the opportunity. But my soul stirred when I heard the voice of God.

Let me encourage you—never follow your senses over the voice of the Holy Spirit. That's what animals do because they haven't been given the breath of life. They sniff the ground for direction. But you are a living soul, a child of the eternal God. And you are led by His Spirit.

## Know Your Purpose

*Follow the Holy Spirit, not your senses.*

# Day 23

<hr>

## COMING THROUGH THE FIRE

And there shall come forth a rod out of the stem of Jesse, and a Branch shall grow out of his roots: And the spirit of the LORD shall rest upon him, the spirit of wisdom and understanding, the spirit of counsel and might, the spirit of knowledge and of the fear of the LORD.

Isaiah 11:1-2

When I saw the school property God had led me to, I immediately recognized that He was giving me an incredible opportunity. But a dark cloud blocked my vision. My friends didn't bear witness with where God was taking me. The voice of my inner prophet got weaker and weaker; and before long, I was experiencing full-blown fear.

I was going through an extremely hard time, and God was testing my commitment to His will. I lost my vehicles and walked to the church. I'd been evicted from my apartment, my credit cards were either defunct or in collections, and companies garnished my check for unpaid loans. After tithes and offerings, I had only $6.40 per week for myself.

No one invited me to preach. Every door closed. Friends soon stopped associating with me. And my enemies loved to see me being destroyed. I was stripped of everything, so that Jesus became the cornerstone of my existence. That's when He took me to Isaiah 11:1-2 and I took hold of the seven things that equipped me to walk in the fullness of my anointing.

1) I understand what the *Spirit* is decreeing to me and I can *rest* in Him. 2) His *wisdom* reveals what I need to do. 3) He gives me *understanding* of how I should do what He commands. 4) He blesses me with supernatural *counsel* and confirms my path. 5) The *spirit of might* guards my soul and assures me of victory. 6) The *spirit of knowledge* gives me specific insight. 7) The *fear of the Lord* keeps me from allowing the enemy any place in my life.

Now I truly understand Christ as the stem out of Jesse…because from the root of divine relationship with Him, I'm watered by divine purpose, connection, and impartation. I have learned that even in the dead of winter, through Him I can bear fruit. If I keep my eyes on Him and delight in His law, He'll bring me out of midnight into a new day.

Let me encourage you. Never be discouraged about your present situation when God gives you a prophetic word—because when He tells you that you're going to come out and increase, you'll come out with more than you've ever had…more than you've ever known.

Yes, it was a struggle to look at someone driving a Mercedes Benz when I had to walk, but I learned how to celebrate Him, and that was worth it all. Fire brings His wisdom, which always leads to greater glory and victory.

## Know Your Purpose

*Even in the dead of winter, through Jesus, you can bear fruit.*

# Day 24

POSSESSING THE LAND

The LORD thy God shall bring thee into the land whither thou
goest to possess it, and hath cast out many nations before thee.

Deuteronomy 7:1

Despite dire circumstances, I submitted a proposal for the
use of the school property. The board placed an ad in a local
newspaper for any other parties that might be interested,
which reveals a prophetic principle: As God leads you into
soul prosperity, He'll present you with an opportunity to
move on something first. Soul prosperity begins with
obedience, and I recognized that I had to obey the
opportunity God was giving me.

I was fearful because I didn't have any resources. I had to
see myself always prospering in the things of the Lord,
*foreseeing* what God was *going* to do. I opened prayer services at
a hotel. My father came for a visit, and I took him to the
property, which now was in a state of decay and abandonment.

God had spoken to me to propose an offer of one million
dollars. After my father walked around the grounds, he said,
"You know, if I was making an offer for this particular
building, for what I know you could do with it, I'd offer them
a million dollars." Without saying a word, I got in the car.

In November they sent my proposal to the Emergency Control Board. I looked for other locations, just in case the approval process took longer. Then I met a realtor who had had interaction with many of the top churches in the area. I asked discreetly, "What do you think about the school building on Ridge Road?"

"I know three companies that have bid on it, and they all have the money to pay for it in cash; so it's sold already." I was resigned that if three companies had the ability to pay in cash, who was I to bid with only a word in my soul? Still, I asked a few people who had been attending our prayer services to go into intercession.

At the board meeting, they revealed that seven companies had submitted bids, and three could pay cash. I had made the first bid. I prayed, "If this is Your will, Lord, You've got to produce it."

The board then announced, "We have selected the vision of Pastor Weeks." They had approved the vision I'd presented instead of those who had "big" deals and cold cash!

The Lord reminded me of His Word to me in Deuteronomy 7:1. He had perfected my journey and confirmed that I was walking in His path to abundance by giving me the land and casting out the other companies. Hallelujah!

## Know Your Purpose

*Opportunity comes to everyone but waits for no one.*

*Act on the opportunity!*

# Day 25

A NEW DAY OF DIVINE INCREASE

Being confident of this very thing, that he which hath begun a good work in you will perform it until the day of Jesus Christ.

Philippians 1:6

From childhood I was creative, wanted more, did more, pursued more, and didn't let anything hold me back. When my bid on the school property was accepted, God began to birth another level of accountability in me, where I had to follow through on a new level of relationships, dialogue, and networking.

I absolutely knew that God was expanding me beyond my horizons. I didn't know how to run a 54,000-square-foot complex and the required security, staff, and engineers. I had to hang around people who did and learn. And I still had to overcome some personal dilemmas.

If you're currently facing a dilemma or your life is dysfunctional, it's because God is testing whether or not you'll let that thing control you. I was about to give up the prophetic word inside me, until I realized that whatever stopped me from fulfilling my destiny would become my god. So I learned to let some things go and let God be God. My father laid his hands on me and blessed my new assignment, and I plunged forward.

When God speaks a "soul word" to you regarding your destiny, you must come into complete alignment with His vision, call it what He has named it, and maintain the proper focus. This path will lead you into soul expansion. God's vision is so big that you must rest in His shadow and let Him guide you.

Created in the image and likeness of God as spirit, soul, and body, you must keep your spirit conscious of God, your soul aware of what He's calling you to do, and your body cognizant of the world around you. God's in the process of revealing to you who you really are; He's helping you find and fulfill your purpose.

God is also going to bring you into divine order. You'll begin to have charge over your house. The anointing on your life will begin to fall into accountability to prove your areas of strength. He's birthing something inside of you. He's shaping a new image that will continue to sharpen into spiritual integrity and divine increase. You will learn to hearken diligently unto the Lord from the prophet of your soul, because it's been echoing into your being everything God wants you to accomplish.

The Lord will not quit on you until you have accomplished everything He has ordained for you to accomplish. Therefore, I pray and believe and decree by faith that you will walk in the power of your soul prosperity and see divine increase.

## Know Your Purpose

*Soul prosperity begins with obedience.*

# Day 26

~~~~~

## LET NOT THE LAW DEPART
## OUT OF THY MOUTH

This book of the law shall not depart out of thy mouth; but thou
shalt meditate therein day and night, that thou mayest observe to
do according to all that is written therein: for then thou shalt
make thy way prosperous, and then thou shalt have good success.

Joshua 1:8

Moses' death marked the beginning of a new season of
destiny. He had obeyed God's commands and taught the people
how to prosper in their souls. Now God re-established the
principle of soul dominion by setting Joshua as the new leader.
He would take Israel across the Jordan River into the Promised
Land. Joshua became the new prophetic prototype for the next
level of soul prosperity—corporate wealth and abundance.

Moses had walked with God, and Joshua had walked with
Moses. That is why Joshua received the new assignment. You
see, when God's overshadowing process is complete and you
have not departed from His Word, you come out filled with
His wisdom—and that's when you're ready to declare the
Word of the Lord. Joshua's faith had been perfected, so he rose
to a corporate anointing and was given charge over Israel.

Nevertheless, Joshua faced a dilemma. He had served as
Moses' assistant for many years. He had been on Mount Sinai

with Moses for forty days and nights. (Ex. 24:13–18.) Joshua knew that God spoke to Moses face to face. But would God be with him as He had been with Moses?

Some of us get stuck thinking that only one person can minister to us, give us the Word of the Lord, or issue the charge to go forward. So the Lord repeated, "Moses isn't going to come back, so you need to arise and do what you've been ordained, prepared, and assigned to do. Go over this Jordan— and make sure you go over with purpose and passion you had the first time" (when he spied out the land).

Here's a prophetic principle: If you're going to possess what God has promised, you must believe His Word and not let go of it no matter what you see, hear, or experience. You have to meditate in His Word day and night and not let it depart from your heart and mind, regardless of what's going on in your life.

A lot of people try to name it and claim it, but the problem comes when they're not saying what God has revealed in their spirit and what they have received by their soul. They have departed from God's Word, their soul doesn't prosper, and what they've been naming and claiming does not come to pass. But when the Word of God is heard in our spirit and received in our soul, our words are full of the power and purpose of God and His will is fulfilled in our lives.

## Unlock Your Abundance

*To possess what God has promised, believe His Word and don't let go of it—no matter what you see, hear, or experience.*

# Day 27

## GOD'S TEST OF LEADERSHIP

Verily, verily, I say unto you, He that believeth on me, the
works that I do shall he do also; and greater works than these
shall he do; because I go unto my Father.

John 14:12

Joshua stood at the dawn of a new era, and God was
challenging him to rise up and take dominion authority. It
would be Joshua's *second* time to cross the Jordan—the
number of divine *agreement*—so it was a prophetic symbol
that something powerful was going to be released.

Don't hesitate when God gives you a commandment,
especially when He's allowed you to see your destiny before it
happens as He did Joshua. Let's say God gives you the
opportunity to sit at a desk that could be your next promotion.
Don't act like you're not supposed to sit there if He's already
allowed you to taste and see! It's time for you to possess it!

Here's the prophetic principle: You have to arise in God in
order to accomplish what other people think is impossible.
Like Joshua, you have to arise in faith, obey His command, and
cross the river. I believe the reason God can't bless many
believers is that we're not willing to go over the Jordan alone.
We're not willing to be the first one over. We want others to
touch, agree, and believe God with us—and that's fine,

because there's power in agreement. However, it doesn't replace the fact that each one of us is required to hear, obey, and diligently pursue our own assignment. Are you willing to hear His command and Go? Will you arise in the prosperity of your soul and become a leader?

God can bless you beyond what you're able to imagine and take you into new realms of prosperity. He will cause strange things to happen by allowing something to get into your spirit that you can't shake. Why? Your soul knows your next level. That's why God begins to transfer things to you when you don't even think they're yours.

Now let me ask you a few things. Do you believe that you can do even greater things than Jesus did? Do you believe God can use you to teach others about Him, heal the sick, cast out demons, or speak in heavenly languages? Do you believe that you can come through whatsoever is testing your faith right now? Do you think, *Jesus was able to do that; I can't* or *Jesus had that authority, and He gave it to me too?*

Here's a prophetic principle: Jesus walked with God. If you walk with Jesus, you can rise up in the prosperity of your soul, activate these same promises, possess true wealth and abundance, and do the greater works!

## Unlock Your Abundance

*When God gives you a command, act immediately.*

# Day 28

~~~~~

## OPERATE IN THE PLACE OF
## YOUR DIVINE ASSIGNMENT

From the wilderness and this Lebanon even unto the great
river, the river Euphrates, all the land of the Hittites, and unto
the great sea toward the going down of the sun, shall be your
coast. There shall not any man be able to stand before thee all
the days of thy life: as I was with Moses, so I will be with thee:
I will not fail thee, nor forsake thee.

Joshua 1:4–5

This verse reveals one of the biggest problems in the
church today. Many of us aren't in the place where God has
given us authority. We're not operating in our divine
assignment. We're struggling against divine impulse and
traveling our own path, sensing what God wants but doing
our own thing. We have a sense of destiny but struggle against
it, destroying what God created us to build.

I exhort you—don't struggle against divine impulse. Give
up your will and surrender to God...because when you begin
to walk in the place of your assignment, nothing will be able to
prosper against you all the days of your life! Settle it that no
matter what, you're going to follow God's path to abundance.
Then whatever people say or do against you won't prosper
because you're walking in obedience. Threats and insults can't

reach the throne of God but fall back down to where they came from; and one day, they'll be put to ashes.

This reveals a vital prophetic principle: When God calls you to an assignment that will fulfill a covenant promise, you're going to stand against opposition. It's not going to be easy, because the enemy will do everything in his power to abort it. If you're an entrepreneur, this means nobody is going to encourage you but you. You have to be strong and very courageous, because what you're doing is not only going to affect your pocketbook, it's going to change the economy, provide people with jobs, and help others possess what God has for them.

This is why God told Joshua to be courageous *three* times and to meditate His Word day and night. The prophetic principle this reveals is that you must speak the Word over yourself to possess what God has given you. I can hear God saying, "Keep My Word in your spirit, and every time you come to a crossroads, you'll start speaking the right thing. They'll criticize you, bring up your past, and remind you of your weaknesses and shortcomings. So stay in My Word because it reflects who you really are."

Your soul must prosper before anything else can, but it cannot prosper if you are in the wrong place at the wrong time, thinking and believing contrary to God's Word. It is critical that you know your assignment, stick to it, and say and do what God says in His Word. Then your words will release the creative power of God to manifest all He has already given you.

## Unlock Your Abundance

*Work in the place where God has given you authority.*

# Day 29

---

## THE POWER OF YOUR WORDS

And I will give unto thee the keys of the kingdom of heaven:
and whatsoever thou shalt bind on earth shall be bound in
heaven: and whatsoever thou shalt loose on earth shall be
loosed in heaven.

Matthew 16:19

The "keys to the kingdom of heaven" are in your mouth.
James 3:8 says, "But the tongue can no man tame." Nevertheless,
Jesus—the living Word—can do it supernaturally. If you submit
to Him as Lord, He'll use your mouth to unlock the victory in
areas you never thought were possible as you speak His Word.

Your words can become rivers of living water that
somebody else can drink. They can bring somebody's spirit
back to life. Your words can quicken someone who's suffering
from spiritual dehydration and cause them to see and do the
will of God. And this is why Joshua had to rise to the challenge.

Joshua learned to line up his communication with what
God was speaking. Let's look at Joshua's commands from the
perspective of the prophetic code. *First* he declared that Israel
would cross over the Jordan to possess the land. *Second*, he
sent spies into Jericho. *Third*, when the spies returned, he
commanded the people to sanctify themselves. *Fourth*, the
priests were to carry the ark of the covenant before the people
into the Jordan.

Joshua's *fifth* command was for Israel to gather and hear the Word of God (grace). *Sixth* (the number of man), he commanded Israel to cross the Jordan. *Seventh*, after Israel crossed over, which *perfected* their journey, he commanded representatives of the twelve tribes to place a stone as a memorial to what God had done. And his *eighth* command brought in the *new day*: "Joshua therefore commanded the priests, saying, Come ye up out of Jordan" (Josh. 4:17).

Before Joshua could lead Israel into the Promised Land, he had to cross over from despair into the joy of the Lord, from doubt into absolute faith, from timidity into being strong and courageous…and a nation was birthed into a new day. Joshua crossed over in his soul by speaking and obeying all God had said to him before he crossed over the Jordan. The rivers of living water flooded his soul and came out of him to flood the souls of the children of Israel so they could successfully cross the river.

You can walk in the divine authority God intended for His children from the beginning—just cross over into a new day. Cross over into your destiny by believing and speaking God's Word—prospering in your own soul so that God can use you to help build a nation. As you declare His Word, you'll make your way prosperous and your words will give life to many.

## *Unlock Your Abundance*

*Let God use your mouth to speak His words to unlock
the victory in areas you never thought possible.*

# Day 30

## Fight to Possess Your Inheritance

Think not that I am come to send peace on earth: I came not to send peace, but a sword.

Matthew 10:34

When Israel crossed over the Jordan, it not only marked a change in leadership, but also a change in divine strategy. God wanted them to multiply but in a different way. He had overshadowed them and prospered their souls; now He was commanding them to take dominion and increase their wealth. And it was through warfare that they would take the land.

This reveals an important prophetic principle: It's vital for believers to come into ownership, to possess more land. When you lease an apartment, you have to abide by the owner's rules; when you own it, you set the rules. So it was vital for Israel to possess the land in order to fulfill their covenant with God unhindered.

I believe because Adam never had to pay the price to take the Garden, he didn't understand what it meant to possess the land and therefore easily lost it. So God required Israel to play an active role in obtaining their inheritance. The prophetic principle here is this: *You value what you invest in.* You take better care of the things that you've worked hard to acquire. You guard and manage them carefully.

As a result, the new season for Israel was a call to constant warfare to take and maintain rule. They had faced enemies before crossing over, but now it was going to a new level. Joshua received strategies for waging war and Israel became a nation of divine warriors. You see, when they crossed over, the shadow of the Lord lifted—and their enemies could see they were coming (Josh. 5:1; 6:1). They actually started to track Israel's exploits, so Joshua needed to call upon God daily for wisdom to be effective, victorious—strategic—in battle.

Many believers are shocked when they discover their call to faith is a call to warfare. But when you get saved you've entered the realm of warfare because you now have corporate responsibility. As God's child you have something to accomplish—and it's part of the bigger picture. You have become an active part of the wealth of the nation. You are interdependent. You have become one with other believers—because certain battles require pulling all of our resources together.

Israel was ready for battle even before the priests came out of the river! So here's the prophetic principle: To possess our inheritance, we must learn how to receive the strategy of the Lord and fight for what He has given us.

## Unlock Your Abundance

*As you move from prospering your soul into taking dominion in your promised land, expect and watch God's strategy for increasing wealth to change.*

# Day 31

## A Divine Pause

But all the people that were born in the wilderness by the way as they came forth out of Egypt, them they had not circumcised.

Joshua 5:5

Israel was ready to fight, but God stopped them to set some things in order. He commanded Joshua to circumcise the men. He wanted to cut a new covenant with a new generation for a new level of soul prosperity. When they obeyed, He told Joshua, "This day have I rolled away the reproach of Egypt from off you" (Josh. 5:9).

Then the manna stopped, revealing another prophetic principle: A new strategy requires new provision. By eating the food of the land, Israel would be equipped to possess it. Many times we don't understand why God brings some things to an end and keeps other things going, but we have to trust Him. He sees the end from the beginning. So we must keep pace with Him. When He turns, we turn. When He moves forward, we possess what He's put in front of us. And when He pauses, we pause.

In a divine pause God cuts away things that can tie us to the past and keep us from prospering in our soul, like bad habits. I've got a very bad habit. I don't sleep a lot, so when I'm tired, I really snore…loudly. My wife has told me she has to go into another room until the snoring stops. That gave me a choice. I could either pace myself so that I don't snore her out of the bedroom, or keep doing things the same way—and not love my wife the way Jesus loves the church. So I decided to change my flight schedules and break late working patterns to get to bed at a decent hour. I knew that breaking this bad habit would improve our quality of life and take us to a new level.

Bad habits can stop us from prospering because they break our rhythm. They distract our focus. But once we deal with them, reconfirm our covenant with God, and come into focus, we can receive God's divine strategy. We will know exactly what to ask of God and be able to hear Him more clearly.

There are times when you think circumstances have stopped your forward momentum, but God has orchestrated a divine pause to adjust you before you move into a new place. That way the enemy won't find any holes in your armor. By forcing you to deal with bad habits, He's actually causing you to move into realms of the Spirit you didn't think you were ready for. And He's going to bless you more than you can imagine.

## Unlock Your Abundance

*Possess more land.*

# Day 32

WEALTH-BUILDING STRATEGIES

For all the promises of God in him [Jesus Christ] are yea, and in him Amen, unto the glory of God by us.

2 Corinthians 1:20 *[insert mine]*

One of the major dilemmas we face in building wealth is many of us have weak vision and a slave mentality. But there are untold riches in Christ Jesus. Every promise is already done even as our souls prosper in Him. Still, there are keys to unlocking His riches.

Never be satisfied with doing as little as you can. And don't do one thing well and be content to be average at everything else. Diversify your portfolio; build additional skills—multiply! Don't get stuck in the rut of always doing the same thing day in and day out. Create your own opportunity while contributing to the well-being of others. Step up to corporate wealth and abundance.

Think ownership. Apply for a loan to start a business. Then the families in your community can be blessed by the excellent services and jobs you provide. Great people create vision because God is a visionary. No one can create like Him! He's been coming up with creative strategies since the beginning of time—why not listen to Him?

If you hearken unto God's voice when He wants to create something new through you, it will turn your world into a new and better place. Only you must be willing to go beyond your comfort zone. Are you broke? Then get a broom and find a store with a lot of leaves and trash in the parking lot. Before anybody shows up for business, clean it up, sweep all the debris way to the back, and don't charge anything. Tell them, "I'll keep this place immaculate…if you pay me this amount per week, I'll paint, clean, and even serve as your parking attendant." You've crossed over into corporate anointing—you're going beyond your boundaries—taking ownership of little so that God can entrust you with much.

I hear the voice of the Spirit declaring new things in three major areas that can revolutionize the church as we know it. First, by applying sound business strategies under the direction of the Holy Spirit, many believers will become debt free. Second, God's going to move us into ownership of property—to the extent that we can divide it with others.

Third, we must take the limits off God—lose our measuring sticks because with what God's getting ready to do, they're going to be too short anyway! Then we will hear His strategy for success. We must not stop short because we don't understand exactly how everything's going to play out…but move forward creatively, knowing all His promises are ours.

## *Unlock Your Abundance*

*Hear and act on God-given strategies.*

# Day 33

―――∿∿∿―――

## LEGAL ACCESS TO WEALTH

> But thou shalt remember the LORD thy God: for it is he that
> giveth thee power to get wealth, that he may establish his
> covenant which he sware unto thy fathers, as it is this day.
>
> Deuteronomy 8:18

It was definitely a new day. Israel was conquering
kingdoms and walking in corporate wealth and abundance—
because they'd obeyed the voice of the Lord. Israel had gained
legal access to the wealth of the nations by following God's
written Law by faith. They remembered Him.

In Genesis 17, God made a covenant with Abraham when
he was ninety-nine years old. Prophetically, *two nines* not only
represent *divine agreement,* but also a *double birthing* (being
reborn or born again). God promised Abraham the land of
Canaan as an inheritance under the condition that every "man
child" be circumcised when he was *eight* days old (*eight*
represents a new day). Israel would be *reborn* (the first *nine*)
before they took Jericho and possessed the land of Canaan.
Later Jesus Christ would give the eternal kingdom to all who
were *born again* by receiving Him (the second *nine*).

Why is circumcision significant? Genesis 17:13 says, "And
my covenant shall be in your flesh for an everlasting covenant."
So God gave His Word in their flesh to equip them to prosper.

Later, Jesus came in human flesh to cut the better covenant, and all who trusted in Him would live an abundant life.

Before dying on mount Nebo, Moses gave the Law a second time. "And he gave Joshua the son of Nun a charge, and said, Be strong and of a good courage: for thou shalt bring the children of Israel into the land which I sware unto them: and I will be with thee. And it came to pass, when Moses had made an end of writing the words of this law in a book, until they were finished, that Moses commanded the Levites, which bare the ark of the covenant of the LORD, saying, Take this book of the law, and put it in the side of the ark of the covenant of the LORD your God, that it may be there for a witness against thee" (Deut. 31:23–26).

A supernatural impartation of strength and courage was released from Moses to Joshua, giving Joshua the ability to uphold the Law. This was his legal access to wealth. Why? Keeping God's Law causes soul prosperity, and when you prosper in your soul, you prosper in all areas of your life.

If you worship God, obey His commands, and work honestly, diligently, and faithfully—you will prosper. This is your legal access to wealth because you are allowing God to establish His covenant in the earth through you.

## Unlock Your Abundance

*When you prosper in your soul, you prosper in all areas of life.*

# Day 34

——*mm*——

## MENTORING OTHERS IN THE BIBLICAL PATH TO TRUE PROSPERITY

> Ye know that the princes of the Gentiles exercise dominion over them, and they that are great exercise authority upon them. But it shall not be so among you: but whosoever will be great among you, let him be your minister; And whosoever will be chief among you, let him be your servant: Even as the Son of man came not to be ministered unto, but to minister, and to give his life a ransom for many.
>
> Matthew 20:25–28

Many people today suffer from a lack of mentorship. And few are willing to invest the time to help others find the biblical path to true prosperity. We must value the people God has entrusted to our care and oversight. Joshua recognized Moses' leadership because he could *see* Moses' walk was *real*. Moses was accountable to God. So Moses could boldly say, "Joshua, you're going to be my minister."

This reveals a prophetic principle: People who are called to lead and be mentors have to step up and be accountable! Moses couldn't sit around, doing what he wanted to do…undisciplined, and then expect to raise up a Joshua to lead a nation to possess their inheritance.

When I neglect my duty to mentor others, it can be equated to spiritual abuse. Study Luke 12:42-47. Mentorship is a vital part of the corporate anointing; so much so that Jesus assigned a harsh penalty for those who take it for granted. Please hear me on this: The church cannot be trusted with material wealth until we learn to value *true riches—people.*

Mentorship releases generational destiny. God commanded Israel to diligently teach their children the same laws they were to follow (Deut. 6:6-7). Early wealth training builds corporate anointing and establishes the groundwork for wealth. These children followed Joshua into the Promised Land and became warriors for God.

A good mentor will make a pervasive impact on your life. A good mentor is thorough and will challenge you to learn all there is to know about your area of focus—and then encourage you to learn other things. A good mentor will reinforce the gift until you've mastered it. Mentorship takes time and discipline—and that's why so few truly embrace it.

Mentorship follows the pattern of Jesus, releasing a corporate anointing that never stops flowing. It's unlimited because it's eternal. And it's a call to greatness. When God calls you to be a mentor and to be mentored, He'll challenge you to redefine yourself and tap your potential, to follow through no matter what's happening or what people think of you.

Be strong and very courageous—and celebrate your next level of discipline. God is empowering us by challenging us to abide in His Word and then mentor others to do the same.

He's building the wealth of His people, and you can't become wealthy by yourself. You can inherit money and become rich, but you can't generate wealth without working strategically with others. So today ask God who you are to mentor and pray for someone to mentor you.

## Unlock Your Abundance

*Value the true riches—people.*

# Day 35

## THE DECISION TO PROSPER IS YOURS

Behold, I set before you this day a blessing and a curse; A blessing, if you obey the commandments of the Lord your God,...And a curse, if ye will not obey the commandments of the Lord your God.

Deuteronomy 11:26–28

God has placed a world of opportunity at our fingertips, but we must choose to follow the right path. Soul dominion and prosperity are conditional. Yes, God does give us the power to gain wealth, but it comes with a warning: "Beware that thou forget not the LORD thy God" (Deut. 8:11).

Have you ever hit a big pothole and your front alignment starts going off? This happens spiritually. We drive into potholes by refusing to obey everything God commands us to do. "Well, I'm not going to church tonight...I don't feel like praying...I'll read the Bible tomorrow...." Potholes. "Oh no, here comes another offering plate...I gave last week; I'm not giving tonight." Potholes. And then you wonder why you keep running off the road! Your wheels are wobbly; they're turning out of control. You blame it on the devil—but you haven't made the right choices.

You have a choice...and whatever you allow to master you becomes your god. In the Garden, Adam chose to eat the forbidden fruit and allowed the serpent to master him. So Adam and Eve lost their prosperity by making the wrong choice.

Soul prosperity isn't based on what you have but on who you are and how you relate to your heavenly Father. Are you rich toward God? Then you're in the place where God can bless you. If not, it's time to examine your soul. Are you obeying His Word and Spirit?

Just like Adam and just like Israel, you have to choose whom you will follow. The generation of Israelites under Joshua chose to serve the Lord and continued to magnify Him after achieving great wealth in the Promised Land (Josh 24:31). This "born-again" nation had kingdom vision, and they handled their wealth according to God's covenant laws.

Let me encourage you today. Even if you've made costly mistakes, God can lead you back to true abundance. He didn't give up on Israel, and He won't give up on you—but He will challenge you to prosper your soul. As His child you've inherited true riches and abundant life in Jesus Christ. He's going to complete what He started in you, but you have to obey the laws of His kingdom and abide Him.

Give everything to Jesus today. Bow your heart to Him and do whatever He tells you to do from this day forward. Like Israel, you will possess your inheritance and prosper in all areas of your life because you have chosen wisely.

## Unlock Your Abundance

*Use the world of opportunities that God has placed at your fingertips.*

# Day 36

ABUNDANT LIVING BEGINS
WITH SOUL PROSPERITY

Therefore if any man be in Christ, he is a new creature: old things are passed away; behold, all things are become new.

2 Corinthians 5:17

Jesus is the essence of soul prosperity, the complete snapshot of everything God is to man—the second Adam—the one who completed the path of soul dominion. During His ministry on earth Jesus demonstrated that He could reference God on every dimension: past, present, and future. He existed in eternity and was born into the earth—and His soul was perfect, timeless…and joined to the Father.

Jesus came in the form of God and took on the likeness of man. He was the shadow of God, shaped to resemble man. And His strength is made perfect in our weaknesses (2 Cor. 12:7–9). He is the first fruits of the Father—the perfect living soul—the life who is the light of men (1 Cor. 15:22-23; John. 1:4). He is Lord, forever worthy to be magnified.

In Mark, chapter 12, the scribe discovered it was true when he repeated the commandments Jesus had just spoken: "Hear, O Israel; The Lord our God is one Lord: And thou shalt love the Lord thy God with all thy heart, and with all thy soul, and with all thy mind, and with all thy strength…" (Mark

12:29–30). He got saved that day. That's why Jesus told him, "Thou art not far from the kingdom of God" (Mark 12:34).

The scribe wasn't far from receiving the promise because Jesus allowed him to see the kingdom. Remember John 3:3, "Except a man be born again, he cannot see the kingdom of God"? The scribe saw because he'd been saved. "If thou shalt confess with thy mouth the Lord Jesus, and shalt believe in thine heart that God hath raised him from the dead, thou shalt be saved. For with the heart man believeth unto righteousness; and with the mouth confession is made unto salvation" (Rom. 10:9–10).

And that was the difference. The scribe could now magnify the Lord and receive the promises of God. The faithful of Old could only believe unto righteousness (see Heb. 11:39–40), but the scribe could confess Jesus and receive salvation. He was now in position to prosper in all areas of his life because his soul was prospering in the Lord.

We must never lose sight of this primary prophetic principle: Our soul begins to prosper the moment we are born again, and as it prospers we enter into the abundance of life Jesus died and was resurrected to give us. We must never take our salvation for granted because it is the key to everything else in the kingdom of God.

## Unlock Your Abundance

*Prosper in your relationship with the Lord.*

# Day 37

A New Day, a New Praise

I will bless the LORD at all times: his praise shall continually be in my mouth. My soul shall make her boast in the LORD: the humble shall hear thereof, and be glad. O magnify the LORD with me, and let us exalt his name together.

Psalm 34:1–3

King David magnified the Lord by faith, knowing he'd inherit the promises in the future. Now hear me. "Continually" (Ps. 34:1) and "whatsoever" ("And he shall be like a tree planted by the rivers of water, that bringeth forth his fruit in his season; his leaf also shall not wither; and *whatsoever* he doeth shall prosper" Ps. 1:3) work together. When *whatsoever* you do prospers in God, you've entered into *continual* praise.

On the other hand, when you lose your praise, it reveals that your soul has lost its fellowship with God. Your soul was created to seek Him, to communicate with Him. Your spirit is still communicating with God about what you've taken to Him in prayer when you sleep. And without that communion, your soul does not prosper and your heart cannot rejoice.

Recognize these times as a time of pruning. Sometimes your "belly" feels sick because you're going through growing pains. Your spirit is trying to get rid of old (dead) things in your soul. God is purging you, getting things out that can't be there on the next level. So you wake up with sickness, dizziness, and depression…not realizing that pain is part of the pruning process.

Why are the humble glad? Why do they have joy? They know that pruning produces much fruit…and it yields abundant prosperity. We must understand the meaning of 1 Peter 5:6: "Humble yourselves therefore under the mighty hand of God, that he may exalt you in due time." When you get down low enough and can still declare, "Nothing's going to stop me from getting in position to know my God," you can celebrate in everything because your soul's already prospering in God. Your humble soul has the joy of the Lord.

Rejoice when you're humbled—because God's going to do something supernatural when you get up! Get 2 Corinthians 4:8–10 *into your spirit*: "*We are* troubled on every side, yet not distressed; *we are* perplexed, but not in despair; persecuted, but not forsaken; cast down, but not destroyed; always bearing about in the body the dying [*cutting*] of the Lord Jesus, that the life also of Jesus might be made manifest in our body" (*insert and emphasis mine*).

You have to be humbled to enter continual praise. And believe me, the new day that comes because you've allowed yourself to be pruned and fine-tuned by the hand of God will be something to shout about!

## Unlock Your Abundance

*Recognize the times of pruning to produce fruit.*

# Day 38

~~~

## A SUPERNATURAL DELIVERY

For with God nothing shall be impossible.

Luke 1:37

When the angel Gabriel told Mary she was going to conceive Jesus, Mary responded, "How shall this be, seeing I know not a man?" (Luke 1:34). This confirms that our minds can't handle what God is doing supernaturally. We wonder, "How can this be, seeing that I don't have the right education...I only make this much a month...I've always been labeled this or that?" Here's how: "And the angel answered and said unto her, The Holy Ghost shall come upon thee, and the power of the Highest shall overshadow thee" (Luke 1:35). It's a supernatural delivery!

God also told Mary she was not alone. "And, behold, thy cousin Elisabeth, she hath also conceived a son in her old age: and this is the sixth month with her, who was called barren" (Luke 1:36). Elisabeth had conceived in her old age—past her time of having children—so she understood what Mary was going through. She was also contending with the miracle power of God.

"And Mary said, Behold the handmaid of the Lord; be it unto me according to thy word" (Luke 1:38). Mary didn't hesitate, and neither can you. When the Word impregnates your spirit, don't wait around for confirmation. Mary didn't ask her sister, "Did you see the angel?" No, she went straight to Elisabeth's.

Elisabeth had already conquered *six* months when Mary arrived. In the prophetic code, *six* is the number of *man*, which means she had come past the opinions of men. The baby was not hidden but visible. Elisabeth was supernaturally carrying a child with supernatural power.

When you respond to God like Mary and Elisabeth did, don't get mad when people can't see what God's doing inside of you—because one day your birthing will come. You have been ordained for this. Something new is being worked in you and you can rejoice.

Too many try to "get the joy" without doing anything for God. Elisabeth had to carry her baby for six months before she got a taste of joy! The prophetic principle is this: Real joy carries you through the last three months of your birthing! It strengthens you to carry the weight of the burden God has placed upon you. Joy equipped Jesus to endure the cross (Heb. 12:2); especially during the overshadowing period between the *sixth* and *ninth* hours, when He finally gave up the ghost. Let's examine the numbers: Man (representing number *six*) was reborn (representing number *nine*), and nine minus six equals *three,* representing resurrection, completion, and wholeness. The supernatural delivery was finished!

## Unlock Your Abundance

*Remember that other people can't see what God is doing inside you.*

# Day 39

~~~~~

## PROCESSING TO PERFECTION

> But the Comforter, which is the Holy Ghost, whom the Father
> will send in my name, he shall teach you all things, and bring
> all things to your remembrance, whatsoever I have said to you.
>
> John 14:26

Adam was given the breath of life at the beginning of time
(see Gen. 2:7). Jesus—the way, the truth, and the life—"gave up
the ghost" when He died on the cross and said, "Father, into thy
hands I commend my spirit" (Luke 23:46). So the Holy Spirit is
the "breath" of "Life" *and* the breath of Jesus Christ.

Before He was crucified, Jesus told His disciples that the
Holy Spirit would return. The Holy Spirit magnifies the Lord
Jesus Christ. And if we're filled with the Spirit, we can magnify
Him. That's how prosperity was birthed in Adam, and that's
how it came back to earth through the second Adam. Let me
explain from a different perspective. When Adam lost his
inheritance, he had been unfaithful in his earthly dominion, so
he lost the breath of life…he lost the Comforter. Then Jesus
prospered in His soul and restored our eternal inheritance,
giving us back the breath of life.

In John 7, Jesus told the Pharisees, "If any man is suffering
without the Comforter, receive Me into your heart and you'll
receive the *breath of life.* You'll recover the dominion Adam

lost when Life left his soul. If you come to Me, you can become a living soul again and enter My rest" (author's paraphrase).

When the Comforter came on the day of Pentecost, the process of perfecting the church began. God is perfecting His church through the work of the Holy Spirit. Through His vital power we are able to walk out God's purpose in the earth. Through the Holy Spirit the Word is "quick, and powerful, and sharper than any twoedged sword, piercing even to the dividing asunder of soul and spirit, and of the joints and marrow, and is a discerner of the thoughts and intents of the heart" (Heb. 4:12). The Holy Spirit executes your salvation, seals your divine inheritance, and puts you in the process of perfection.

Jesus—the living Word—is discerning your heart right now. He saved you to the uttermost and the Holy Spirit reconnected the eternal heart of God with your mortal heart, which is why you can govern your soul through the power of the Holy Spirit. You now have soul dominion because the Holy Spirit—the breath of life—lives within you. The Comforter has come to empower you and to perfect you in Christ. Through Him rivers of living water can flow out of you to be His witness and impact the world around you. Hallelujah!

## Unlock Your Abundance

*The Comforter comes to empower you and perfect you in Christ.*

# Day 40

***

## Magnify the Lord Together

O magnify the LORD with me, and let us exalt his name together.

Psalm 34:3

Let's make room for Jesus in the heart of our souls...and magnify Him together. Satan attacked the corporate anointing bestowed upon Adam and Eve, and they lost their inheritance. He divided them and conquered. He slithered over to Eve and asked, "Yea, hath God said?" The enemy did not know God as Lord, so he couldn't even say the word. That's why it is important for us to magnify God as our Lord and to not be divided as Eve was from Adam. Let us magnify the Lord together!

Here's a final prophetic pattern. In Moses' Tabernacle there were three levels: the Outer Court, the Holy Place, and the Most Holy Place. Now humor me while I illustrate this prophetic pattern.

You're standing with others in the Outer Court, having just come into the knowledge of Jesus Christ as Lord—lifting up praises to God. He causes you to magnify His lordship by teaching you to worship Him in Spirit and in Truth. You begin to move closer to Him. Another believer begins to draw closer to God also, and you touch in agreement. Both of you are now magnifying the Lord.

Then God draws you into the Holy Place. At this new level you magnify Him even more and begin to prosper your soul. Everyone there begins to unite in corporate agreement and the prophetic cycle intensifies. Your partner from the Outer Court moves into the Holy Place, and when you touch and agree again on this level, God draws you both into the Holy of Holies.

You now love Him with all of your heart, soul, mind, and strength…and you love your neighbor as yourself. You praise, exalt, and magnify His name as He fills you with His power and glory—your soul arises in the abundance of divine prosperity and corporate anointing.

Everyone magnifies the Lord together and celebrates with those who've been blessed to go before them. God perfects you as you magnify Him, and you possess your eternal inheritance in God as He releases you into the fullness of His kingdom. You arise declaring His words in completed soul dominion. And whatsoever you do is blessed, even as your soul prospers.

What's the prophetic principle? Everybody who's seeking the kingdom of God will embrace the corporate anointing. This is true prosperity. This is soul dominion. It's also why God expects our souls to prosper. So choose *this day* soul dominion; choose to magnify the Lord individually and corporately. Then, *as your soul prospers,* everything that God bestowed upon Adam in the beginning…*will be yours.*

### Unlock Your Abundance

*Prosper your soul through praise.*

# Prayer of Salvation

God loves you—no matter who you are, no matter what your past. God loves you so much that He gave His one and only begotten Son for you. The Bible tells us that "...whoever believes in him shall not perish but have eternal life" (John 3:16 NIV). Jesus laid down His life and rose again so that we could spend eternity with Him in heaven and experience His absolute best on earth. If you would like to receive Jesus into your life, say the following prayer out loud and mean it from your heart.

*Heavenly Father, I come to You admitting that I am a sinner. Right now, I choose to turn away from sin, and I ask You to cleanse me of all unrighteousness. I believe that Your Son, Jesus, died on the cross to take away my sins. I also believe that He rose again from the dead so that I might be forgiven of my sins and made righteous through faith in Him. I call upon the name of Jesus Christ to be the Savior and Lord of my life. Jesus, I choose to follow You and ask that You fill me with the power of the Holy Spirit. I declare that right now I am a child of God. I am free from sin and full of the righteousness of God. I am saved in Jesus' name. Amen.*

If you prayed this prayer to receive Jesus Christ as your Savior for the first time, please contact us on the Web at **www.harrisonhouse.com** to receive a free book.

Or you may write to us at:

**Harrison House**
P.O. Box 35035
Tulsa, Oklahoma 74153

# ABOUT THE AUTHOR

Thomas Weeks, III is a bishop, prophet, conference host, and highly sought after motivational speaker. He is Co-founder and Bishop of the Global Destiny Christian Community along with his wife, Senior Pastor Dr. Juanita Bynum Weeks, headquartered in the Washington D.C. metropolitan area.

A socially concerned entrepreneur and educator, Bishop Weeks has spearheaded several community service organizations, the Internet's Destiny Network, and is also establishing Destiny University. Bishop Weeks studied Mass Communications at the University of Delaware, holds a Bachelor of Arts degree in Theology, and is pursuing advanced studies toward a Master of Arts in Christian Counseling at the Christian International College of Theology.

MINISTRY INFORMATION

Bishop Thomas Weeks, III • P.O. Box 60866 • Washington, DC 20039

Executive Office:
Ministry Office: 202-829-4151 • Facsimile: 202-829-4153

e-mail: Info@MyGlobalDestiny.com
Website: www.MyGlobalDestiny.com

To get your *FREE* MP3 download of Thomas Weeks, III speaking the exciting principles in this book directly into your life, log on to his Website for his *Instructional Guide to Soul Prosperity:*
www.myglobaldestiny.com/eaysp

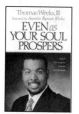

If you've enjoyed this mini-devotional and want more teaching on how to prosper your soul and your future, *Even As Your Soul Prospers,* the book on which this shortened teaching is based, will draw you into even deeper relationship with the Source of true prosperity and all things good.

*Even As Your Soul Prospers*
ISBN 1-57794-710-X

Available at your local bookstore.
www.harrisonhouse.com

EMPOWER YOUR LIFE
WITH SUCCESS FOR DUMMIES

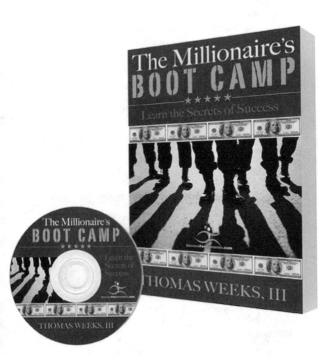

To find out more about Bishop Thomas Weeks, III
please visit us on our Web site at
www.myglobaldestiny.com